# Thinking Outside the Box, but Living Inside the Lines!

by Dr. Benjamin S. Akins

DORRANCE
PUBLISHING CO
EST. 1920
PITTSBURGH, PENNSYLVANIA 15238

The contents of this work, including, but not limited to, the accuracy of events, people, and places depicted; opinions expressed; permission to use previously published materials included; and any advice given or actions advocated are solely the responsibility of the author, who assumes all liability for said work and indemnifies the publisher against any claims stemming from publication of the work.

Dorrance Publishing Co
585 Alpha Drive
Suite 103
Pittsburgh, PA 15238
Visit our website at *www.dorrancebookstore.com*

ISBN: 978-1-6442-6960-2
eISBN: 978-1-6442-6312-9

I dedicate this book to my children:

Christopher, Joecicario, Jelocka,
Tatiana, and Devante Akins.

Nothing means more to me than being a father. It is the greatest responsibility I have and cannot be relinquished. I appreciate the value you add to my life. You are my world.

# Thinking Outside the Box, but Living Inside the Lines!

❋ "I am *motivated* by the thoughts of my own mind, *challenged* by what others believe to be impossible."

❋ "*Motivation* is the driving force or reason by which one is inspired or compelled to act. Consequently, motivation is not a cause, it is an effect; its seed is in itself. The seed is *motive*."

❋ "*Motive* is the purpose that generates active energy and creates what is motivation. Therefore, motivation is predicated on *motive* being the source of inspiration that produces positive energy."

❋ "Accepting a *negative* reality and leaning on it to justify misbehavior is sometimes a choice made to keep from doing what you know needs to be done. It becomes an excuse to remain as you are."

❋ "Own your happiness and work your way into the place you have dreamed of being."

❋ "Live each day *with* purpose, *on* purpose."

❋ "Always challenge a person's mindset with *truth*."

❋ "Do not speculate, seek *facts*. Do not trust theory, seek *truth*. Do not guess, seek *knowledge*. Do not assume, seek to be *better informed*. Do not doubt, seek *answers*. Do not rush to judgment, seek *clarity*. Do not be skeptical, seek *good information*. Do not settle, seek to be *empowered*. Do not be a 'know it all,' seek to be *educated*."

❋ "Belief is a powerful principle yet it is often susceptible to a degree of subjectivity. Therefore, a wise man substantiates his beliefs with *truth*."

❋ "A strong belief without the support of *truth* is as unsinkable as the *Titanic*."

❋ "At times, there is no rhyme nor reason, and the only thing that keeps you grounded is *principles*."

❋ "Daily wickedness as an evil habit of the mind is to make an *illegitimate* source a *legitimate* option."

❋ "It matters when *it* matters."

❋ "Be careful not to fall in love with *potential*. On the scale of productivity, what a person *does* will always outweigh what they have the potential to do."

❋ "*Vision* is the place where circumstance is most contradictory."

❋ "Develop your disciplines in the simplest of things, for the day will come when it gets complicated and *discipline* will be the difference."

❋ "When you *know* what to do, *do* more of it, *long enough*."

❋ "Thinking a thing does not create a thing, it influences what you speak. Speaking a thing does not create a thing, it influences what you do. *Doing* a thing creates a thing and works to transform your habits. It is those habits done consistently over time that shapes your character and determines your destiny."

❋ "Your past is the past, if you leave it there."

❋ "The *solution* is simple; the *discipline* is difficult."

❋ "It is okay to *reflect*, just not long enough to *relive*."

❋ "Everyone makes mistakes; therefore be quick to forgive. Forgiving does not excuse misbehavior. Forgiveness frees the forgiver. It empowers you with control of the potential *negative* responses to what has been done."

3

❋ "*Information* without *application* is like knowing the answers to a test, but not writing them down."

❋ "Life is like a long road trip to your destination of choice. Always know where you are but concentrate on your *destination* and the *time* it takes to get there."

❋ "Some people are so accustomed to the struggle, unfortunately, it has become the basis of their expectations."

❋ "The most valuable lesson I have learned from my past is to spend more time in the present with an intentional concentration on my future."

❋ "Own your decisions; future generations are depending on what you decide."

❋ "Who you are is a sum total of your experiences, and decisions made in the past. Who you will be is the result of lessons learned from it that influence but should not hinder your way ahead. *Learn* from it, do not *lean* on it."

❋ The *birth* of a nation has always followed the *death* of a people."

❋ "Life is full of tough decisions. You have to be even tougher at times to make them."

❋ "I have failed enough for my own good; cried a little, made my share of mistakes, and poor choices; had a number of heartbreaks and broke a few hearts along the way as well, but I am still here. I acknowledged it, learned from it, decided to do better and did so. This is the *secret* of my success."

❊ "Keep moving forward. Shifting from drive to reverse generally happens after you stop."

❊ "A *healthy* diet will never consist of *forbidden* fruit."

❊ "Learn from your mistakes and do not make the same mistakes twice. The key is making the lessons learned about *you* and not so much about the situation. When situations change, if *you* have not changed as a result of what you have learned, there is a tendency to repeat the same behavior. However, if *you* have changed, you are in a better position to handle any situation."

❊ "Do not assume you know it all or what you have mastered is the only way to do something successfully simply because it has worked for you. Adaptability is a necessity; things are constantly changing."

❊ "It is not always about finding a better way. Sometimes, it is just about learning another way."

❊ "It is not enough to *know* what to do; *do* what you know."

❊ "Learning + Repetition = Retention."

❋ "Successful people did not do everything right; they *survived* everything they did wrong."

❋ "When you truly see the *value*, it is easier to count up the *cost*."

❋ "Imagination is not the issue; the struggle is finding a means to bring all you can imagine to life."

❋ "In America, not much has changed. Unfortunately, what we see are new ways of doing more of the *same ol' things*."

❋ "You are not failing; it is called *succeeding slowly*. Persevere; do not give up."

❋ "The greatest struggle for those in Christ is the contrast between *who you are* and *who you used to be*."

❋ "A genuine *apology* for a deed done yesterday is the *fertilizer* for a seed sown today; without it there may be no harvest."

❋ "Your past has passed; let it go."

❋ "The God of heaven gives each of us the *power* to get wealth. The *power* of the mind, the *power* of a belief system, the *power* of the spoken word, the *power* of success principles, the *power* of a product, the *power* of a network, the *power* of leverage, and the *power* of duplication, all of which are within our *power*."

❋ "Being *broke* is about economics; being *poor* is about *mindset*."

❋ "Today's Choices Shape Tomorrow's Memories."

❋ "What is worse than not *knowing* what to do? *Knowing* what to do and not *doing* what you know."

❋ "The key to success is principles not necessarily methodology."

❋ "Things happen, but *forgiveness* prevents negative feelings and emotions from sticking and staying."

❋ "The essence of a well-balanced life is strongly dependent upon human consumption, naturally and spiritually. The discipline of diet directly contributes to one's growth and development. Therefore, the principle associated with the Holy Scriptures is the power behind every spoken Word. The uniqueness of God's gift given to those entrusted to teach these principles is their perspective."

❋ "All men and women are created *equal*, which speaks to human value by the standard of *heaven*."

❋ "Consistent positive interaction breeds emotional ties."

❋ "A self-inflicted wound is harder to forgive, because many times you know a more responsible decision could have been made."

❋ "Choose wisely; making a decision is often much easier than living with one."

❋ "A fearful mindset is the anchor that keeps your greatest dreams from sailing."

❋ "A hurtful experience is like garbage. *Forgiveness* is the process of bagging and putting garbage in the dumpster for disposal. On the contrary, *unforgiveness* leaves garbage exposed and allows it to fester. In a short period of time, *if you do not forgive*, you end up with flies and maggots as well."

❋ "I am a king in the 'jungle' called *life*. I wake up every morning eager to go *lion* again."

❋ "Choices are the result of our *intent*, but *intent* seldom dictates *outcome*."

❋ "Learning is the result of constant exposure to new information. Feed your mind as much and as often as you feed your body."

❋ "The ultimate goal of practical knowledge is the practice itself or its productivity. Knowing what to do, *theoretically*, means little without the discipline to do, *practically*, what you know to do."

❋ "The reason many are unsuccessful at time management is in reality, we cannot manage time. We cannot speed it up, slow it down, nor stop it. The goal in life should be to master good *self-management*. Self-managers have learned to make good use of time."

❊ "Since theoretical knowledge aims at no other purpose than knowledge itself, *behavior* becomes the barometer by which we measure the character of an individual."

❊ "The gift of *free will* is never given without guidelines that govern human behavior."

❊ "What matters more than what other people think? Knowing it does not matter what other people think."

❊ "No matter where you are going, know *who* you are following."

❊ "What can you do you have not done? What can you stop you have not stopped? What can you change you have not changed? What can you say you have not said? What can you forgive you have not forgiven? What can you read you have not read? Who can you help you have not helped? Who can you visit you have not visited? Who can you text you have not texted? Who can you call you have not called? Who can you thank you have not taken the time to thank? Who can you apologize to you have not rendered an apology? Who can you pay you have not paid? Where can you go you have not gone? Where can you sow you have not sown? Where can you serve you have not served? Where can you give you have not given? Where can you allocate time, while you have time to allocate? Do not wait until tomorrow—you have a lot to do and an undetermined amount of time to do it. You can manage a number of things in life but TIME is not one of them. Use the time you have to become a better *self-manager*."

❋ "The spoken Word creates, brings forth, blesses, unlocks, and gives access. It also reprimands, requires, restricts, curses, and condemns."

❋ "Greatness is often the result of being willing to follow directions *before* you see where you will end up. *Go* then *see*."

❋ "When purpose and power align in faith the impossible is probable."

❋ "Only *once* in the history of eternity did *'The Father'* do something so strenuous and time consuming it required rest: *CREATION*. Therefore, whenever your creative ability is on display, understand the work required will be arduous and the end result will take time. *Evening and morning*; there is always a process."

❋ "In order to succeed, do not focus on what *'some say'*; concentrate on what you can *imagine*."

❋ "We have all been through something; make your *next* move your *best* move."

❋ "It is easy to tell the story when the story is easy to tell."

❈ "Four rules to live by: 1) quote Scriptures correctly, 2) always seek the first intended meaning of Scriptures, 3) never attempt to quote a Scripture you have not read, 4) never take for granted something taught is Scripture."

❈ "Many people want the things you want, but some have permanently accepted where they are and what they have as their ceiling."

❈ "You are what you take the time to become."

❈ "When you are blessed to receive what you do not deserve *return the favor*."

❈ "Do not *'make it up'* to someone; do what you say you are going to do the first time."

❈ "Think about what you are thinking about."

❈ "Violence is the essence of Retaliation."

❈ "If you want a *heavenly* response to spring out of you, sow the seed of the Word of God within you."

❈ "If you could do something about what you have not been able to do something about, would you do it?"

❈ "What do you want? Who can you count on? Where are you headed? When is the right time to act? Why are you not where you want to be? How do you change the course of your life? Many people can relate to asking the same kinds of questions, and praying for answers. However, the answers are many times shrouded in opportunities. The question is, if given the opportunity of a lifetime, would you seize it in the lifetime of the opportunity, or find every excuse to remain where you are?"

❋ "Never underestimate the *value* of an invitation."

❋ "The *healthiest* way to give back to your community is to give the people in it and amazing *opportunity*."

❋ "What are you *doing* with what you have? In the end, what you *have* is never more significant than what you are *doing* with it."

❋ "It is often surprising what some people run *from* when you see what they run *toward*."

❋ "I long for the day when it does not take the *worst* in America to bring out the *best* in America. It should not take tragedy to reset our moral compasses to True North."

❋ "Do not be concerned with not knowing; be concerned with not knowing."

❋ "In the game of tug-of-war, if a person is not pulling *with* you, it is best for them not to have their hands on the rope."

❋ "Very few people care about your story unless you win. That is why you must *win*, period."

❋ "People make *references* to losers; for winners, they make *documentaries*."

❋ "When purpose and power align with vision and action, prosperity is produced."

❋ "With everything in life there is a *process*; within the process is the *grind*."

❋ "Discipline is *knowing* what to do and the *willingness* to do it even when you do not want to."

❋ "With every comment you make, every opinion you share, every email you send, every text or social media message you post, you *introduce* or *reintroduce* yourself to the world. Be mindful of the things you *say*."

❋ "A person can have knowledge, skills, and abilities, but if they are not *coachable*, it may be in your best interest to let them play elsewhere."

❋ "Speech is *free*. However, it is the *words* you choose that *cost* you."

❋ "Greater good seems to only be accomplished by the things a person *does* and not necessarily by what a person *knows* or *says*."

❋ "I would rather see someone doing something wrong, trying to do something right than not doing anything at all; it is an easier fix."

❄ "Everyone has an opinion, and that is okay, but realize your opinion says more about *you* than it does about the subject of conversation."

❄ "Tools work best when you know how to use them."

❄ "Anything worth being *said* once is worth being *heard* more than once."

❄ "In coaching, be reasonable. Being *reasonable* requires two things: 1) knowledge of the standard, 2) knowledge of the situation. Always have a standard, but very few, if any, rules. Standards establish order and empower a coach to exhibit sound judgment as much as is appropriate, fair, or moderate depending on the situation. A rule, in an effort to establish order, predetermines the outcome without consideration of the situation and ultimately takes control away from a coach, in their own system."

❄ "If you choose not to choose, you have made a choice."

❄ "Theory always leaves us with a question, but the God of heaven provides the conclusive."

❄ "The key to *success* is making the success of others more important than your own."

❄ "When others doubt, take it upon yourself to become the evidence."

❋ "Who you run *with* will not only determine what you run *from*, but also what you run *toward*."

❋ "Negative references in the Scriptures must be fulfilled, but it does not have to be by *YOU*."

❋ "Sometimes attrition is a part of growth and elevation to the next level."

❋ "It is difficult to rise up when you are carrying dead weight."

❋ "Here is a start; *STOP STOPPING*."

❋ "It is what you *do* after you say '*AMEN*' that is the difference maker."

❋ "Time *unused* is time you *lose*."

❋ "Few people see the work. It is what you do behind the scenes that determine the results seen by everyone."

❋ "It is difficult for someone to develop a healthy opinion of you when everything you say about yourself is unhealthy. If you are *not* positive about yourself, why should someone else be?"

❋ "Do not expect people to accept you, like you, love you, or think highly of you, if your *story* reads like a poorly written manuscript. Remember, *you* are the author."

❊ "Something to always keep in the *front* of your mind; nothing kept *'in the back of your mind'* will assist you in character development and decision-making."

❊ "There is a huge difference between those who love the *game* and those who love the *grind*."

❊ "Follow your passion; it is not enough to dream."

❊ "When there is nowhere to hide, *know* where to hide."

❊ "*Intellect over emotion* is much more than a choice; it is a concept. When the concept is met by commitment, it easily becomes a way of life."

❊ "When you look at life, *time* is not running out; *your* time is running out."

❊ "The big picture is what you see but never forget *clarity* is revealed in the little things, which it consists of. So, just when you think you have seen it all, look again."

❊ "You have been given the gift of time. What you *do* with it must be worth your *immortality*."

❊ "The perfect picture is not about being picture perfect."

❊ "You can do what you want at your house, but *what* you do will determine if you will ever receive an invite to mine. If you miss the message in that statement, you may miss *heaven* as well."

❋ "One day you will be forced to go at it *alone*. The person who loved you, appreciated you, rode with you, walked with you, talked with you, believed in you, encouraged you, cheered for you, listened to you, poured into you, stood by you, saw the best in you, tolerated the worst in you, and wanted the best for you will be *gone*."

❋ "Though death is unfortunate, it is always final. You can hold on to the memories of those you love but you must let them go. There will be no life for the person, who continues in a relationship with death. Consider this, when you visit the cemetery, you remain by the gravesite only so long as you continue to remain. When *YOU* decide it is time to go on with your day, you put one foot in front of the other until you are on your way. That is the point of emphasis. One step at a time, but you must first decide *'it is time to go.'* You can always make a return visit; just remember *you cannot stay*."

❋ "The true goal is not to win, but to become a *winner*. Winning is what you sometimes do; unfortunately, so is losing. Being a *winner* is who you are. It pays to know the difference."

❋ "You do not have tomorrow; tomorrow is a dim expectation until it happens, but when tomorrow becomes today, now it is time for action and forget about yesterday. So, stop making excuses and make a difference. Too many people have become extremely good at what they were *going* to do."

❋ "An individual who throws stones and hides his or her hands is a coward."

❋ "Though faith is often misconstrued it is rather conventional in its daily application. Faith is the basis, foundation, or confident expectation, which is present, tangible, and upholding those things hoped for. In other words, it is in one's confident expectation or anticipation that the face of faith is revealed. Hence, faith literally becomes the evidence of things not seen."

❋ "This year, *just do it*. Anything you were *going to do* last year did not get done."

❋ "The greatest tragedy of life is to die without ever truly living."

❋ "Always know who, what, when, where, why, and how; those are the *basics* of clarity."

❋ "If you could go anywhere in the world, where would you go? If you could see anything in the world, what would you see? Saying it is always the easy part; there must be a means to an end."

❋ "When there is nowhere to run, *know* where to run."

❋ "Great things will happen *tomorrow*, not merely because I said it, but because of today's *sweat equity*."

❋ "Some of the simplest concepts make the biggest impact."

❋ "All it takes is vision. You cannot *consistently* hit a target you cannot see."

❋ "Many are called but few are those, who have made a *choice*, a *commitment*, and a *vow* never to quit."

❋ "There is no specific pathway to success. Success is a *principle-based philosophy* that requires each individual to commit to a level of excellence regardless of the endeavor. There are a number of alternatives, or pathways to choose. Still, the success principles are relatively the same. Therefore, it is not the path one chooses that results in success, but rather a set of principles when applied properly and consistently over time increases one's chances to succeed."

❋ "What do you do when some doubt, others question, loved ones refuse to listen, friends lack faith, and few show support? *Do it anyway.*"

❋ "When you look in the mirror, what do you see? You see, a *reflection* of you. Understand, the mirror has no conscience, no opinion, no mind of its own; it cannot lie, give compliments, nor make insults. The mirror can only *reflect* what you project. The way you feel about what you see is an issue you can control. The power of true reflection is within you. Display in the mirror what you desire to see; be it and you will see it. You may lie to yourself, but the mirror will always *reflect* the truth."

❄ "The game of strategies and uncertainties can be so intense a play clock is instilled to govern the amount of time you have to decide between plays. Be decisive; the clock is running. Wins are not achieved by your strategy alone; S.M.A.R.T. action must be taken."

❄ "Just because you set a good example does not mean you will be liked, loved, or even appreciated, for that matter. Some people have a million reasons why they cannot do what is required to succeed, when all they truly need is one reason why they can."

❄ "When you master the little things, *BIG* things happen."

❄ "Sometimes the best way to show you love a person is to leave them."

❄ "When you set the example, do not be surprised if some people are intimidated or even offended by the standard you set. They will sometimes refer to you as a *'showoff,'* when what you really are is a *model* of how it should be done."

❄ "Do not expect some people to be happy with you or for you. Those who could do more wish you would do less. Why? Because your success is a constant reminder of their untapped potential as a result of their excuses, procrastination, stagnation, or lack of commitment."

❋ "Just because a person has a voice and a platform does not mean they are saying things worth listening to. Be careful who you allow to pour into you."

❋ "It is not so much what is *poured* into a person, but what is *planted* that makes the difference."

❋ "What you know is what you know, but what you *do not* know is what you *do not* know. Always be willing to learn."

❋ "When there is nowhere to turn, *know* where to turn."

❋ "There is no magic. It is really simple, *DO NOT CHEAT YOURSELF.*"

❋ "Move forward in life like you travel: *NO EXCESS BAG-GAGE.*"

❋ "Be responsible for your attitude or be held accountable for failing to do so."

❋ "Constant correction and force of will instills discipline."

❋ "Many times you get out of a situation just as you got into it, one decision at a time."

❋ "Do not look for others to believe in you, encourage you, support you, cheer for you, pray for you, pray with you, follow you, or be there for you. Do not waste time *talking* to other people about what you want or what you are *going* to do—instead, look in the mirror and talk to *yourself*...every day, then *GO DO IT*."

❋ "Do not draw conclusions for others. The emphasis in counseling should not be what you say, but what you cause an individual to realize. *Realization* empowers a person with the necessary tools to bring about positive change."

❋ "If a small investment and the work involved could change your life forever, how difficult would it be to convince yourself it is worth it?"

❋ "For many, the truth is hard to hear and sometimes even harder to accept."

❋ "Truth can be like medicine; it may not taste good going down, but it is good for you."

❋ "Not all people embrace the value of sound advice, corrective criticism, or a need for change. Some are more receptive of generalizations as opposed to specifics. Generalizations leave room for anonymity. Specifics demand personal accountability."

❋ "The essence of psychology is not linked to a particular moment in time. It is the *totality* of cognitive reasoning that reshapes historical philosophies and evolves into modern-day models."

❋ "Being the best at *what you do* is sometimes a hindrance to being the best *you can be*. It is a matter of *ability vs. capability*."

❋ "No one is *perfect*, but that is not an excuse to be *imperfect*."

❋ "A contemporary psychologist in all of his or her wisdom is certainly not brilliant to the point of being exclusive in their conception of psychology. It is necessary to always compare the present to the past, *in its proper context*, so as not to diminish the value of historical concepts."

❋ "When did the *uninformed* become experts in what they know nothing about? Be careful who you take advice from."

❋ "If the *goal* is to win, then *prepare* to win. Without a commitment to *proper preparation*, winning is not a realistic objective."

❋ "Winning consistently creates a winner's mindset. If you want to accelerate the process, you must increase the number of opportunities to win. Set more holistic goals: economic, emotional, psychological, physical, spiritual, and social. The more goals you set, the more opportunities you have for winning to take place. The more winning takes place, the more your *belief* strengthens over time, thus raising your *confidence* to achieve unbelievable goals."

❋ "If the goal is to win consistently, you must become unbreakable."

❋ "Pushing yourself is necessary but pushing yourself *too hard* is not the goal. There is a difference between *going hard* and *going overboard*."

❋ "Winning is great, but *how* you win is equally important."

❋ "Losing is inevitable; therefore when it happens, lose like a winner."

❋ "Stop saying you want to *win*, if you struggle with a negative mindset, negative attitude, mismanagement of emotions, lack of confidence, lack of focus, lack of concentration, laziness, lack of commitment, or the need to make excuses. Start by saying you want to *change*, then do so."

❋ "Perception is reality to the one who perceives."

❋ "Many people struggle with execution because they never truly intend to follow through. *Developing* a plan or *setting* a goal is simple because it does not require discipline."

❋ "Our belief system is the byproduct of our teachings."

❋ "Attitude is the byproduct of our belief system."

❋ "When the God of heaven breathed the breath of His image *(Spirit)* into mankind, man became a living soul or the living image of the Father. It is easily understood in this regard: one breath from Eternal-Life, we became life; one breath from Omniscience, we became knowledgeable; one breath from Omnipotence, we became powerful; one breath from Love, we became loveable; one breath from the Creator, we became creative; one breath from the Spirit, we became spirit; one breath from Faith, we became faith-based beings; one breath from Eternity, we became time. The power of the divine impartation from the God of heaven released a measure of His divine attributes into His now *'earthly representational image.'*"

❋ "Always acknowledge the feelings and emotions of others but do not allow it to override the *principles* that govern good decision-making."

❋ "Emotions are healthy as long as you can manage them."

❋ "If something is not working, do not be afraid to change your approach yet maintain the common principles of success."

❋ "Leaders do not seek to clone; they educate, elevate, and empower others to be the best version of themselves possible."

❋ "Some people *lose* so much they cannot handle winning. Others *win* so much they cannot handle losing. Both extremes are a detriment to true success."

❋ "The principle of *positive energy* is the wind beneath your wings; do not just fly, SOAR."

❋ "Develop the leaders around you. By doing so, delegation becomes a valuable stress reliever."

❋ "Make up your mind to *progress,* not *regress.* You are either moving forward or going backward; no one remains the same."

❋ "We live in an opinionative world where many are influenced by perception, theory, hypothesis, idealism, tradition, and philosophy. Therefore, it becomes extremely difficult for sincere individuals to fully grasp the concept of absolute truth."

❋ "The toughest thing about really wanting to help people is accepting the fact not all people really want the help."

❋ "Leadership is a beautiful thing; remember, what makes you a leader is the fact that people have chosen to follow you."

❋ "Whatever you worship is ultimately what you end up serving."

❋ "Perception is the manifestation of what is perceived; it is the way a person sees something or someone, which is a postulation of reality; that is why it is called perception."

❋ "True leaders recognize the ability in others and work hard to *maximize* it, not *manipulate* it."

❋ "Spirituality without education is as dangerous as education without spirituality."

❋ "Training wheels do not teach a child how to ride a bike. They prevent a child from injuring themselves until they learn how to ride. However, left on too long, training wheels hinder the natural process of learning."

✻ "Training wheels help a child to manage the *fear* associated with incompetence, while he or she improves on the little things that lead to success. Many times, over your lifespan, you will feel like that child."

✻ "Leaders must be calculated with words. Be intentional and make use of well-thought-out responses. Words can develop or destroy."

✻ "Do not allow some people to *'love you to death.'* Realize when some people's version of *'love for you'* is literally a death sentence."

✻ "You may have heard the old cliché, *there is no 'I' in team.* However, there is great value in embracing the individualities within a team rather than trying hard to eliminate it. Just as *there is no 'I' in team* there are no teams without *individuals.*"

✻ "Many people are interested in *what* God said, but *why* and to *whom* He said it, is equally important."

✻ "Anything taught has the potential of being mastered."

✻ "Even *progress* can become a distraction. Celebrate it, but never lose sight of your goal."

❃ "Good Presentation + Good Conversation = Good Representation."

❃ "You want to be good, but good is not a guarantee."

❃ "Perception is perception; reality is reality."

❃ "Make your expectations clear. Do not assume people know and understand what you have not properly conveyed."

❃ "It is never wise to *assume* in a relationship when it is possible to simply *ask*; your assumptions could be wrong. You must get out of the habit of thinking you *'know'* a person well, and the longer you have been with someone, the more tempting it is."

❃ "There is a thin line that separates *what we are* from *who we are*."

❃ "Free will is a gift from the God of heaven; as long as it is *lawful*, how others choose to exercise it is none of your business."

❃ "Thoughtfulness has no price tag; it is the *value* that counts."

❃ "It is not just *what* you do but *who* you do it with that makes the difference. It is the *who*-factor that transforms a group into a team."

❃ "Fear of turbulence is the reason many people choose not to take flight."

❋ "Many people would do more if they knew more."

❋ "Following does not suggest a relinquishing of one's individuality. It is a matter of submission, not control."

❋ "Never want anything so bad you make bad decisions to obtain it."

❋ "Mentors differ from leaders. Leaders take a position out front, because it is about the destination. Mentors take a position alongside, because it is about development. Mentoring is more intimate than leadership."

❋ "If you ask the God of heaven for something in faith, does it matter how, when, or through whom He decides to answer you? If so, it may be the reason you are on the waiting list."

❋ "Stop apologizing when doing better is just as easy."

❋ "We all have limitations; know what your limitations are. However, over-extending yourself reveals your limitations to others and that is unacceptable."

❋ "Do not try to fit in; create space for others to fill in."

❋ "Life is an experience of *impact* vs. *intent.*"

❋ "It is not just important for your team or organization to make adjustments; leaders must adjust, too. One of the more difficult adjustments for leaders to make is to know when they have reached their ceiling in support to a member of their team."

❋ "It is amazing what can be accomplished when it does not matter who gets the credit, and all that counts is the *God of heaven* gets the glory."

❋ "Pray, but filter all decisions using the principles of the Holy Scriptures."

❋ "Be careful how you treat others; God just may select *them* as the mail carrier to deliver the very thing you have been praying for."

❋ "Know when it is time to redirect someone to another source. A great leader knows him or herself, his or her people, and who is fully capable of taking each person to the next level. Humility and wisdom are characteristics needed to point them in the right direction."

❋ "People generally know what they would like to say but struggle at times with how to say it. People know what they would like to do but often seem to find the wrong ways of getting it done."

❋ "A mere profession of faith is not indicative of the possession of faith."

❋ "Once you say what needs to be said, *DO* what needs to be done."

✻ "In decision-making, never get bogged down in your strategy. A successful strategy is always coupled with deliberate action."

✻ "Forgiving others will ultimately determine *what you do*. Forgiving yourself will ultimately determine *who you are*."

✻ "Overcome disobedience and you will cease from sin."

✻ "True leadership seeks to produce a deep hunger for discipleship that creates stronger and more effective leaders."

✻ "Change is not change until change is CHANGE."

✻ "What does it say about your leadership if you delegate something to someone you have not mentored and prepared to complete the task? Be careful when painting a picture of someone else's incompetence; you may be surprised when the portrait bears a strong resemblance to you."

✻ "The greatest threat to forgiving oneself is *guilt*."

✻ "There is a difference between stating a *reason* and making an *excuse*."

✻ "People in need will approach the unapproachable. So, measuring your approachability in a person's time of need is not a good barometer. The best way to know if you are approachable is to always leave your door open and if people pop in just because, it is a good sign they feel like they can."

✳ "If your people cannot go to you first, who are they supposed to go to? It means very little if you believe you are approachable yet your people believe you are not."

✳ There is a difference between a *mistake* and a *bad decision*. When you do something, you know you should not do, it is not a mistake, it is a bad decision; own it. It is nearly impossible to forgive yourself for something that is not properly labeled. Take the first step by calling it what it is."

✳ "There is a time given to all things under heaven. No matter what time it is, always know *what time it is*."

✳ "Be consistent in your behavior. Instead of telling others what to do, be so consistent they inquire about what they see you do regularly."

✳ "I know the feeling we sometimes get when people quit. If a person quits on you and thus you quit on them, both of you are *'quitters'* with different reasons for quitting."

✳ "Faith is an absolute, because it proceeds from the divine nature of the God of heaven. Knowing that God alone is the source of absoluteness, anything that proceeds from the divine nature of God is also absolute because the nature of God is God. It is impossible to separate the God of heaven from who and what He is."

✳ "Stick to truth and facts; deal less with feelings and emotions."

❋ "Operate with a balanced and sensible mindset in your actions and responses."

❋ "Get an umbrella for rainy days but build an *ark* for when the rain does not stop. How you prepare for the storm will often determine how you get through it."

❋ "Always listen to what others have to say, whether you agree or not. It is your willingness to acknowledge how they feel that matters most."

❋ "You must be willing to risk failure in order to succeed."

❋ "Master the skill of adaptability. In an ever-changing world, you must be able and willing to reroute, *constantly*, without losing sight of your goal."

❋ "Do not focus on your circumstances or what others believe to be impossible. Make your requests known to God, and when He answers you through opportunities, take action."

❋ "Always be open to new options, but quitting is not one of them."

❋ "At times, you may be misunderstood, misinterpreted, or misrepresented, but it is better than being misguided, misinformed, or misled. Control what you can control. What is about *others* is about *others*; what is about *you* is about *you*."

❉  "The ultimate challenge for each of us is to become the best version of ourselves possible."

❉  "Commit to improving your self-image, self-respect, self-worth, self-esteem, self-confidence, self-efficacy, self-awareness, self-acceptance, and self-actualization. However, true self-mastery will only be achieved with the realization it cannot always be about you."

❉  "Do something you have never done before and do it like you have never done it before."

❉  "Scars tell a twofold story; that, which you have suffered, you have survived."

❉  "Do not expect someone to fall in love with you until you do."

❉  "Read to be inspired and better informed by history. Develop a love and respect for the power of documentation."

❉  "Purpose + Energy & Excitement = Passion."

❉  "Passion is about giving not receiving. Receiving can be the result of passion, if you are involved with someone who is also passionate, but receiving is never the focus of one that exudes true passion. It is always about impartation."

❉  "Always be willing to do the work, even if it is a small percentage of the work; do your part."

❋ "Your network is your net worth, if you can agree on the worth of the work and decide to do it together."

❋ "Learn to compartmentalize crisis; no spill over."

❋ "A positive winning attitude is the result of quality information and proper preparation."

❋ "Success revenge is overcoming the challenges or oppositions of life, which is not always about people."

❋ "You get more done by doing."

❋ "Leadership is the execution of multiple disciplines."

❋ "Your sight is sometimes fixed on someone with no vision."

❋ "Your enemy's attire fits like a tailor-made suit on some of your friends."

❋ "Own the means to providing what is necessary for your survival."

❋ "Good communication is the key ingredient to a healthy relationship."

❋ "There is a difference between *faith* and *belief*; use both respectively."

❋ "Before you carry his seed, be certain he will carry the load."

❋ "There are things we all have in common; doubts, fears, haters, challenges, etc. The key to success is something inside that compels you to keep going. Amazing things have been accomplished by people who look like you and I, but it was not done until they did it. Maybe the level of resistance you face is because of your purpose; your contribution. Push through the process until your selfie has a special place in the bigger picture."

❋ "See yourself as the ALMIGHTY sees you, and allow Him to order your steps. His way always requires more personal growth and development."

❋ "If one month is time given to the celebration of black history, use the other eleven to make it."

❋ "Love a woman, protect a woman, and provide for a woman; it is a man's responsibility. A woman gives life to all of humanity, which is only possible because the first man gave life to her."

❋ "Formal education is so expensive, in most instances, the price of admission requires a negotiation of your freedom."

❋ "Reflect on yesterday, prepare for tomorrow but execution is always about today."

❋ "The secret to marital success is the realization one's position at any given moment is interchangeable without diminishing value."

❋ "No matter who you are, what you do, or what you have, the testimony of your household matters."

❋ "Be selective about your circle. Ultimately, they help determine what gets out as well as what gets in."

❋ "You will never understand that which you do not know. Scrutinize the facts, and uncover the *truth*."

❋ "Outer struggles take a lot to overcome; inner struggles often take a lifetime."

❋ "One of life's greatest challenges is to *like* many of the people you love."

❋ "Social media is a powerful platform; be intentional and deliver a responsible social message."

❋ "Having genuine respect and appreciation for all people does not alleviate my responsibility to address pertinent matters concerning my own."

❋ "What you are believing God for is a clear indication of how much more you should be doing."

❋ "Too many people prefer a handout to a hand up because a helping hand generally requires them to pull."

❋ "Emotional recovery is an uphill journey. Something someone said often speaks louder than what you are saying."

❄ "It does not take a long time to say a lot."

❄ "Loyalty is having my back even when you cannot stand to see my face."

❄ "The best communication is a good response based on effective listening."

❄ "If you want to leave a legacy, be a person of significance."

❄ "Those who never start should consider themselves finished."

❄ "Sometimes greatness is on the other side of *'shut up & listen'*."

❄ "You do not have time to not have time."

❄ "It takes a million dollars to be a millionaire, but only one to no longer be."

❄ "Never evaluate an opportunity through the lens of your challenges; it guarantees an obstructed view."

❄ "In order to win BIG, surround yourself with BIG winners."

❄ "*Help* is a consensual experience."

❄ "With all thy getting, get understanding. Why? Understanding creates self-awareness and a high level of personal accountability. To always do something out of obedience suggests there must first be instruction."

❋ "We are living in a time when *spirituality* can no longer be a theological, philosophical, or psychological concept people struggle with. We are living in a day of practicality; therefore, the goal must be simple. People need relevance and applicability. If the Holy Scriptures do not come to life in such a way people experience spirituality in the simplest forms of everyday living, our chances of salvation are very slim."

❋ "When evil is sown, evil is reaped every time, regardless of who the sower may be."

❋ "It is about YOU. There is a difference between being selfish and making yourself a priority."

❋ "The greatest leaders are the best followers. The key to success is to find someone worthy of following. The *journey* is as important as the *destination*. When the two are conjoined, followers become leaders as a result of the process."

❋ "When you are truly in the fight it is not convenient and never comfortable."

❋ "All men and women are entitled to *equal opportunity* because equality in terms of opportunity is the standard for *human rights*."

❋ "Why has it become *normal* to be *abnormal?* The lines now appear to overlap."

❋ "If you are going through something, keep *going* and *growing*."

❋ "Create a new narrative for the not-so-distant past with every decision you make today."

❋ "What you think cannot be done has been done by someone who refused to accept that thought when it crossed their mind as well."

❋ "Goals generally result in the things we *love*; what it takes to accomplish those goals generally requires the things we *hate*. For this reason, people tend to purpose things they never carry out."

❋ "An unbeliever asked me, *'Why do you believe in God? How do you know your belief is right?'* I paused for a second, since the question has little to do with my position and more to do with the uncertainty of his. After a brief pause, I responded, *'For the same reason I believe the warning label on a gallon of bleach: HARMFUL IF SWALLOWED. I would rather believe in the God of heaven and be wrong than to not believe and be WRONG.*"

❋ "Too many people are afraid to dream because they have been living a nightmare."

❋ "In every generation the people of God have had a battle to uphold the truthfulness of Scripture, and ours is no exception."

❈ "In your daily planning, begin with non-negotiables, then those things that are necessary, followed by those things that are important, then those things that should be done, can be done, and fillers."

❈ "You may believe in the power of prayer but sometimes struggle with the *empowerment* associated with having your prayers answered."

❈ "Some people are like ratite birds; having wings does not guarantee you will ever take flight."

❈ "Thanks to the God of heaven; a little *faith* brings out the BEST in me. Thanks to my doubters as well; a little *doubt* brings out the *BEAST* in me."

❈ "It matters: self-esteem, self-image, self-efficacy, self-worth, and self-confidence. What matters most is how you see *yourself.*"

❈ "In the jungle, *eat* or be eaten. *Survival* is dependent upon your perspective of the *slaughter.*"

❈ "Do not burn a bridge you just crossed. It got you to your new destination even if the bridge was shaky, unstable, and had you scared for your life while crossing it."

❈ "The character of a man is revealed by his choices."

❈ "Wisdom is knowledge and understanding properly applied."

❋ "What is more important than doing what you are told? Doing what you know to do without being told because you understand why it should be done."

❋ *"What doesn't kill you* should be prepared to contend with your wrath in the not-so-distant future."

❋ "Thank the God of heaven for the winning formula: FAITH + WORKS = the *IMPOSSIBLE.*"

❋ "You want to be disciplined when you need to be but true discipline is developed when you do not want to be. Do this enough and when you need discipline, it is there."

❋ "Are you willing to go *first,* then see what He *will* show; what kind of legacy He *will* make; how He *will* bless; how great you *will* become; how much of a blessing you *will* be?"

❋ "The strength of every leader should be the willingness to follow."

❋ "Remember, the end result is never in question as it relates to the promises of God; *HE WILL DO IT.* The end result is a matter of *'if'* and *'when'* you decide to follow directions."

❋ "Not everyone will want to be on your team, and that's okay; there are seats in the stands. If they would rather watch, give them a show."

❊ "*What*—is the principle in building. The compounding effect will reveal *who*, *when*, *where*, *why*, and *how* of the equation. *What* you build is based upon what you are preparing for."

❊ "The largest room in the world is room for improvement; make sure you are always in the room."

❊ "Change for the Scriptures' sake and you will never have to change again."

❊ "One of the greatest gifts a person can give or receive is '*a second chance.*'"

❊ "Understand the *purpose* of prayer; do not pray for things God has given us the *power* and *resources* to do for ourselves."

❊ "Low self-esteem and a poor self-image prevent you from being successful when success is possible."

❊ "Contentment is a degree of happiness or satisfaction with your current state. When you consider the things you have, you find pleasure in your situation with a level of acceptance, if there is no improvement. However, being content does not suggest the absence of aspiration or a desire for better. The difference is your perspective. When the effort to improve is because you believe you can, in an effort to achieve your personal best, that is a healthy perspective. On the contrary, if a desire for improvement is motivated by a selfish motive to be better than someone else or a dissatisfaction with the blessings you have, that is unhealthy and is discouraged."

❋ "God is so *GOD*; good is an understatement."

❋ "Your *destiny* is freely entrusted to your *choices*."

❋ "The Goodness of God is not always good *to* us but is always good *for* us."

❋ "True leaders focus on *people* before profit or personal gain."

❋ "If you have a good education with an excellent job in a great career field, that is *wise*. If you spend time building your own business as well, that is *brilliant*."

❋ "Disobedience is the seed by which ALL sin springs forth."

❋ "Just as you feed your body, you must feed your mind a healthy diet as well."

❋ "Esteem the Word of God above *anything* and *anybody*."

❋ "When you look at yourself in the mirror, be proud of who you see. Realize what you see is not a finished product, but a work in progress. Maybe you are not where some people would like you to be or think you should be. Maybe you are not even where you would like to be, but you are certainly not where you used to be."

❋ "When you cannot seem to move *on*, move *forward*."

❋ "What you put into your body has a lot to do with what you get out of it, and so it is with your mind."

❋ "A message to the doubters and unbelievers: *No Comment Required*."

❋ "It is important to duplicate principles and not merely to copy the behaviors of others. Duplicate the principles of *why* people do what they do; it will cause you to do what *YOU* do consistently."

❋ "What is worse than an absentee parent? An absent parent *in the home*."

❋ "Do not ask the God of heaven for that, which He has promised—walk in *obedience* and *believe it* to receive it."

❋ "We need true leadership in this country, leaders that hear the issues of people and convey the proper message to the masses on behalf of all parties without prejudice or bias, so that order is preserved."

❋ "Where you are now will be your past tomorrow. Therefore, *'The Father'* gives us but *one night* to cry over spilled milk."

❋ "In an effort to turn your life around, turn 180°; a 360° turn is the same direction."

❋ "We are never beyond learning. We must be continuously receptive to the revelatory light of the Gospel."

❋ "When thoughts and beliefs are exercised outside of what is considered *lawful*, justice must be done and executed swiftly without excuses on behalf of the perpetrator."

❋ "The choices of mankind corrupted God's creation. Therefore, the consequences are ours to own."

❋ "Being poor is a *condition of the mind*; staying poor is a *choice*."

❋ "A stumbling block or a stepping stone is a matter of perspective."

❋ "Principles are the power of Scripture. The perspective is unique to each individual gifted by God to feed His people."

❋ "The God of heaven uses imperfect people to perfect people."

❋ "Religious insanity is the attempt to keep manmade rules not supported by the Scriptures."

❋ "It is hypocritical to embrace one philosophy of extremism and oppose another, since both appear to have its roots in the same kind of ideology."

❋ "All it takes is vision. Unless God gives a specific design, we can build whatever we can imagine."

❋ "Financial freedom can *never* be associated with *employment*."

❋ "When the daily requirement is most challenging, never forget we are in the business of service, and service will always ride the wings of great sacrifice."

❋ "Rightly dividing the word of truth is to separate and conjoin truth with truth. It is like putting the pieces of a puzzle together to reveal a portrait. This is strictly for the purposes of understanding principles. However, once the goal is accomplished, consolidated truth can be used to share a healthy perspective with the masses."

❋ "Many people believe in heaven, yet few are making Scriptural preparations to go there."

❋ "Having a job is like pouring a glass of cold lemonade for someone else. Having your own business is taking the time to have a tall, cold pitcher of your own."

❋ "You may do an amazing job leading, coaching, and mentoring your current team, but if you do not continue in your own growth and development, you will not be guaranteed the same success going forward."

❋ "As a teacher of the gospel, it is your obligation to be right. You can always build upon a foundation of truth; just never be wrong. If one masters the principle, which includes first intended meaning, then one's perspective should be sound every time."

❊ "It is time to prosecute the guilty to the fullest extent of the law (regardless of race, record, or profession) and stop blaming the masses on all sides for responding when it does not happen."

❊ "The God of heaven does not do all of the work; He is not supposed to. Your perspective is enhanced by how much additional work, education, and experiences you have. You have the responsibility to ensure your perspective aligns with Scriptural principles; that is your work to own."

❊ "Let all people of color be cognizant of this fact: True progress toward racial justice and equality is to raise the consciousness of other ethnicities, while mastering the art of good communication within our own communities."

❊ "A *team* is only as effective as the *individuals* and coaches that make up the roster."

❊ "Some people are so comfortable with the work of their own hands, they reject even what the God of heaven has prepared as their *next-level blessing*."

❊ "Mind how you treat others. Make *'I'm Sorry'* a seldom used response."

❊ "First intended meaning is within the principles of the Scriptures."

❋ "Personal relationships should not come with perks in business."

❋ "It is good to work hard so your family can live well, but it is equally important to be there *personally* with the ones you work so hard for."

❋ "In the game of life, call your play, and use lessons learned to call your next play. Just remember, success is the proper *execution* of the plays you call."

❋ "Sowing and reaping is a literal concept, as such is the law of cause-and-effect."

❋ "In the average family household, *Peter* is getting the business and *Paul* is living the dream. It is a budget nightmare so many hardworking Americans are accustomed to."

❋ "Many times, you hold a person accountable for things you have not fully expressed to them truthfully. Not only is this unhealthy; it is unfair."

❋ "Retirement is not about age; it is about income. How many people do you know who cannot afford to retire? The 40/40/40 Plan is a systemic illusion. What is your Plan B?"

❋ "Life is business and business is life. Master this concept and create a healthy perspective of faith, family, fitness, finances, fun, and fellowship."

❋ "*All Lives Matter*, though philosophically correct, is far from commonplace in America. It is a concept so many have died trying to make a realization."

❋ "You are stronger than you think. Challenge yourself in ways that make you uncomfortable. The elasticity of your character will reveal new truths about you."

❋ "We have heard enough of the hypocritical nonsense. Concerning racial tension in America, no one side is truly in a blameless position."

❋ "Business and profit are about volume. Every business relies upon a *network* to remain in business."

❋ "Due to biased rhetoric and selective hearing, conflict resolution is not a simple task. Racial issues need to be addressed independently as opposed to being rolled into a collective narrative."

❋ "You are either a part of a network or *responsible* for a network."

❋ "Train the voices in your head to speak a new language. Teach them to sing new songs. Program your mind with a heavenly script and require them to know their lines."

❋ "Compressing timeframes is the result of mastering the *'opportunity vs. time'* concept."

❋ "Ever *forget* what you forgave? It is not required; just stop thinking about it."

❋ "Successful people generally have few issues making money. The biggest challenge for most successful people is *growing* the money they make, intentionally and responsibly."

❋ "Thanks to the God of heaven for our country's independence, and for ALL of us, who have sacrificed so much to make it possible. Respect and appreciation is not merely what is *said*, on days like *Independence Day*, but what is *done* every day. What are you *doing* to contribute to a better America?"

❋ "The God of heaven has given you a natural barometer that applies in most instances of decision-making. When faced with a decision, evaluate your natural responses *first*. Whatever comes easiest, is the path of least resistance, or requires little to no *work* on your part is generally *not* the direction you should take. However, if it requires self-discipline, hard work, character, commitment, principles, morality, ethicality, resiliency, or any of the qualities that suggest personal growth and development, then *that* is a clear indication of what is best for you. In other words, stop making things harder by choosing what is easier *to* you. True success begins with realizing your *comfort zone* is really your *danger zone*."

❋ "When people show you who they are, and sometimes who they are not—believe them. Yes, love them, but do it responsibly by learning to protect yourself."

❋ *"Ofttimes people place objectives right there under* our *noses intended to inspire everyone to succeed*; these are called O-P-P-O-R-T-U-N-I-T-I-E-S."

❋ "Each day is significant therefore do something worth putting your signature on."

❋ "It only takes a few moments and a *responsible decision* to change the course of your life forever."

❋ "People typically allow for justice to prevail, but that is not happening consistently enough for the masses to feel comfortable with trusting the justice system. As a result, it becomes *personal* for many, even if it is improper. When a person sees the reality of a situation and concludes *'the injustice that occurred could easily have happened to them or someone close to them,'* it is no longer considered isolated. It is perceived to be an incident at the front door."

❋ "There is a lot to learn from a *'power couple'* when they stand *TOGETHER*; there is no better way to do it."

❋ *"Blood* makes us relatives, but *relationship* makes us family."

❋ "Ever stop to think, *'What if everything you thought you knew about your significant other is wrong, no longer exists, or is no longer true?'* Been together for some time? Well, consider this; when you look in the mirror today, is it safe to say many things about your outward appearance have changed for the better or worse? If your answer is *yes*, rest assured emotional, psychological, and other *intrinsic* qualities have changed about you equally as much, if not more, over time. Since this is the case, understand it is also the case in the life of your significant other. Very few things about you two are the same as the day you met. So, if *you* are constantly changing, evolving into who you are today, then you must also understand there is a constant need in your relationship for reacquaintance. Do you really *know* the person in your relationship or is it that you *knew* the person, and the person you *knew*, you may no longer *know*?"

❊   "At times in all relationships, it is difficult to truly say what you are feeling or share what is on your mind. The devastating result, in most instances, is the slow deterioration of what is expected to be the most delicate and important relationship in your life. How does this end? Will your partner ever understand? Why is the person you love hurting you this way? Your partner is hearing you but are they listening? These are just a few questions many have asked over the years. Each day manifests the *fruit* of your problems, but when do you find the time and moral courage to address the *root* of your problems? How can you maximize the *'good'* in your relationship (which you do have), while minimizing the less desirable? This is the beginning of a responsible conversation."

❊   "Ignorance is no excuse. You need to examine the truth before you participate in activities, traditions, fads, or what is trending."

❋ "I would rather receive a *'no'* than a *'yes'* with a *'no'* effort."

❋ "Not everyone is leery and questioning. Not everyone is in doubt or unbelief. Not everyone is saying, *'Why me? Why this? Why now?'* Not everyone makes current decisions on past experiences. Not everyone makes assumptions or rushes to judgment when it is possible to get their questions answered. Truth is, not everyone wants to see you successful. Not everyone is willing to show you how to win. If you are happy with your life but not satisfied; if you still have a hunger deep within your belly; if you want more for yourself, your family, and your friends; if you want to upgrade your lifestyle; if you want to leave a legacy, you are not alone. Maybe it is time to accept you are not like the others; maybe (just maybe) you are simply like those who say, *'Why not me? Why not this? Why not now?'*"

❋ "Ever forget what you forgave? It is not required; just stop talking about it."

❋ "There is no independent leader of the free world."

❋ "Consider yourself when pointing the finger at others. *Good leadership* is a simple concept to the one not responsible for exhibiting it."

❋ "The United States will only experience healing when *we* fully acknowledge the pain and issues of all sides."

❋ "Some people cannot stomach your success. You love them genuinely, but secretly they are in competition with you; refusing to be outdone. Jealousy has a distinct dialect. Pay attention to the conversation; verbal and non-verbal. Their love-language is profane, yet you call them a friend."

❋ "Manage your emotions. Damage done by a response in anger is sometimes worse than the offense in question."

❋ "Sometimes your greatest opposition is someone in the same uniform that is not on your team."

❋ "It is better to hurt a person's feelings for a moment, *if necessary*, than to destroy a relationship for a lifetime with silent frustration."

❋ "Ever stop to think the major problems in your relationship are the result of minor changes unrealized?"

❋ "Revelation is when the God of heaven opens up your understanding to who He is, His divine purpose, and His plan of salvation for His people. From there, you move from principles to perspective based on the wisdom and knowledge imparted to His elect."

❋ "There is a fundamental difference between freedom and liberty. One comes with a price, but the other is a gift."

❋ "Everyone is getting older, but not everyone is growing up."

※ "Your test is a testimony in the making."

※ "A *'partnership'* achieved in deception is a setup that makes a breakup inevitable."

※ "Do not let someone else's *doubt* make you question your *belief.*"

※ "Never take thoughtfulness for granted. If you only knew, what a person thought of you to think of you."

※ "The quality of teambuilding is revealed by those around you."

※ "You may not be wrong, but not being wrong does not necessarily suggest you are right."

※ "If you respect someone enough to solicit their advice, it should not be such a struggle to consider the advice they offer."

※ "In order to *go* where many have not gone, you must be willing to *do* what many have not done."

※ "Imagine what can be accomplished, if we decide to work together. It is not a new concept; it is a forsaken one."

※ "The Complete Evolution of Self is a work in progress, *if the work is in progress.*"

❋ "There is a thin line between *planning* and *procrastination.*"

❋ "A good success plan always puts a deadline on decision-making and a high priority on subsequent action."

❋ "Never allow a self-induced holding pattern to develop between *planning* and *responsible action.*"

❋ "A concentration on the welfare of your family should be carried out with calculated actions that ensure your efforts match your expectations."

❋ "The deceptiveness of being *'BUSY'* is an issue that keeps most people from accomplishing meaningful tasks in their daily lives. It is important to evaluate what you are *'busy'* doing and not simply pat yourself on the back because you have a lot going on."

❋ "Your *'next-level blessing'* is about what you do not know; it is THAT information that propels you to the place you have always wanted to be."

❋ "*Formal education* always has an agenda—a concentration, if you will. On the other hand, *self-education* is unconstrained; it allows an individual to grow and develop in ways that are not only holistic but more valuable long-term."

❋ "Quitting is for quitters."

❋ "To center your attention on *'what you do'* is only partially correct. To lose sight of *'who you are doing it for'* is to miss the true essence of what career development/broadening is all about."

❋ "If you see something, say something; just be sure what you say is based on what you see and not what you *think* you saw."

❋ "Allow great memories to become the foundation on which to build exciting new experiences."

❋ "Ignorance is the worst diagnosis known to man."

❋ "Too many people have a first-class desire with an economy-class price point."

❋ "Friends will always be there when the jump is easiest. When it is a leap of faith, be prepared to jump alone, if necessary."

❋ "Learn to accept some people stop following you when they realize you are truly going somewhere."

❋ "Nothing rings louder than silent frustration."

❋ "Many of your greatest fears are the result of your perception, not your reality."

❋ "If you say something you did not mean to say or do something you did not mean to do, follow it with a *meaningful* apology."

✳ "A Message to the College Graduate: The worst thing about being a college senior is the culmination of life as a young adult: *Graduation Day*. Tomorrow, life as you have known it will be no more. Tomorrow is the conclusion of today never to be undone. Tomorrow is the day you realize the true meaning of a moment in time. The essence of memories fully embraced today will someday haunt you. Tomorrow morning is the day you wake up to the normalcy of life full grown. Tomorrow is the day everything matters, and everything counts. No more games to play, for tomorrow you become a pawn in the game of life. Working is the highlight of every day for wages that will never be yours to own. Today, you work because of a desire to have extra money in your pocket, but tomorrow you realize that same pocket now has holes. Today's stresses of young adulthood are transformed into the stresses of daily life as an *adult*. Making ends meet is a daily challenge. Expenses become the flavor of the day, and it is now your turn for tasting. In the game of life, you pay to play, every day. Tomorrow, you will realize—*today*, time was on your side; tomorrow time will be ticking against you. Tomorrow is a new beginning; up early to work longer than you slept, only to lie down a few hours before the next day begins the same routine. Remembering you have so much to do *tomorrow* for others, at the same time recalling the things you forgot to do *today* for yourself. Tomorrow is the day you are no longer a priority even to you. Tomorrow is when you are responsible for everything but the possessor of very little. Tomorrow is when you assume control of a life you have very little control of. Today you are a young adult. Tomorrow you become one of us, looking at life in the past tense, finally realizing just how special of a time it was. Today, society views you through the window of compassion as a college student. Tomorrow those in society will see you as their competition. Today, you have front-of-the-line privileges. Tomorrow you are in a never-ending line waiting, fighting for an opportunity to prove yourself. Tomorrow is when the body begins to break down and the mind never fails to remind you of how things used to be, how you used to look, and used to feel. Today, you look forward to a new year. Tomorrow, you realize the difference a year makes. Today, you are eager to let things go. Tomorrow, you will find yourself clinging, holding on. Today, a smile is easy to come by. Tomorrow, you face the endless road in the pursuit of happiness, yet all of the rest areas ahead of you are full of those gone before yet to reach their destination. This is not a slight against tomorrow, but tomorrow you will realize just how much you miss today. Let me tell you about *tomorrow*, for tomorrow I will not have to tell you anything; it will speak for itself. Tomorrow is coming; there is nothing you can do to stop it. In the meantime, instead of focusing on *tomorrow*, take full advantage of *today*."

❉ "Falling down is a part of life; *getting up* is a part of the process."

❉ "Too many people are comfortable with their complaints, satisfied with sympathy. They do not want help; they want attention. They would rather have pity than to be pushed. They do not want answers; they love acting like there are none. They choose to worry over doing the work. They look for excuses as opposed to following the example. They claim to be tired of the very things they tolerate and many times perpetuate. They seemingly desire success but are not willing to sacrifice. They are quick to forward a chain letter but seldom do things to bring about real change. They love to be heard, but they rarely take the time to listen. They will also be upset with ME for calling a spade a spade."

* "Every champion has been hit, hurt, sometimes knocked down, and in many cases suffered loss. If you are unwilling to absorb your fair share of punishment, you will never be one."

* "Whatever makes you quit or prevents you from ever getting started will never apologize for hindering you from receiving your *'next-level'* blessing."

* "The joy was in the *journey*. It taught me so much about me."

* "I am *finished*, not *done*."